Original title:

Unfurling Quills Within the Mermaid Dust

Author: Kene Elistrand

ISBN HARDBACK: 978-1-80562-717-3

ISBN PAPERBACK: 978-1-80564-238-1

Phantoms of the Inked Mermaid

In shadows deep where secrets sigh,
A mermaid swims, her whispers nigh.
With inked tattoos of tales untold,
She weaves her magic, brave and bold.

Her laugh, a hymn beneath the waves,
Calls forth the hearts of daring knaves.
In moonlit dreams, she twirls and spins,
A dance of light where darkness thins.

Her eyes, like pearls, reflect the night,
A glimpse of worlds where dreams take flight.
With every flick of her cobalt tail,
She tells of journeys through storm and gale.

Yet phantoms linger in coral groves,
Echoes of sailors, their ancient oaths.
In whispered tones, she hears their cries,
The haunting songs of those who lie.

When dawn ignites the sky with gold,
The inked mermaid's stories unfold.
A tapestry of ocean's grace,
Forever bound in this haunted space.

A Maritime Journal of Fluttering Fins

Upon the waves where shadows gleam,
Lives a world woven from a dream.
With fluttering fins that dance with glee,
This journal holds each tale, you see.

In seaweed halls where secrets keep,
The whispers of the ocean creep.
Each entry sings of joy and woe,
Of tides that ebb and winds that blow.

The dolphins play, their laughter bright,
In currents swift, a pure delight.
While hidden realms beneath unfold,
In azure depths, adventures bold.

From coral castles, bright and grand,
To sandy shores where dreams are planned,
Each page reveals a new surprise,
A symphony beneath the skies.

So sail with me through briny mist,
With every flick, a chance not missed.
In this journal, magic brims,
A maritime yarn of fluttering fins.

Starlit Strands of Seaweed Dreams

In twilight's glow, the seaweed sways,
Whispers of dreams in mysterious ways.
The stars above, like lanterns bright,
Guide hidden thoughts through the velvet night.

With every wave, a story untold,
Tales of adventure and treasures of old.
The moonlight dances on ocean's face,
While sea creatures twirl in a fluid embrace.

Drifting on currents, the wishes are spun,
A tapestry woven, when day is done.
Beneath the surface, where shadows reside,
The heart of the ocean, a deep, secret tide.

Each ripple carries a promise anew,
Of magic and wonder in every hue.
In starlit strands, our spirits entwine,
Where dreams and reality gracefully align.

The Alchemy of Ink and Salt

In quiet corners, the ink flows free,
Transforming thoughts like the deep, blue sea.
Pages whisper secrets, both old and bold,
As stories emerge from their ink-stained hold.

With every stroke, a world takes flight,
Crafted from shadows, from day into night.
Salt of the ocean, mixed with the ink,
Creates a potion that makes hearts think.

Through storms and calm, the pen does wade,
Casting spells where dreams are made.
With each drop of ink, the magic is cast,
Binding the future to whispers of the past.

The sea and the quill, a dance so divine,
Together they drink from the chalice of time.
In the alchemy, we find our voice,
In ink and salt, we make our choice.

Beneath the Surface of Forgotten Words

In sunken depths where shadows lay,
Forgotten words long lost the day.
They linger softly, like ghosts that sigh,
Calling to sailors who drift on by.

Each syllable hides in the brine's embrace,
Waiting for seekers to find their place.
The echoes shimmer in the twilight mist,
A tapestry woven with threads of the tryst.

In the heart of the ocean, wisdom sleeps,
Guarded by mermaids, where sunlight weeps.
Hidden treasures, like verses untold,
Awaken the dreams of the young and old.

Beneath the surface, a language of tides,
Where every crest and trough abides.
Unlocking the secrets, we dive in deep,
To stir the waters, where memories seep.

Casting Spells with Nautical Pens

With nautical pens, we weave the tales,
Of ships that conquer the fiercest gales.
Each stroke is magic, a compass's grace,
Guiding the hearts of the brave to their place.

Words like waves, they crash and break,
Each line a voyage, each pause a wake.
The ink flows salty from oceans wide,
Casting spells of wonder, an endless tide.

In the lantern light, the ink glistens bright,
Charting a course through the darkest night.
With every word, we summon the sea,
To carry our hopes, to set our minds free.

The paper unfurls like a sail in the wind,
Launching the dreams that our hearts have pinned.
With nautical pens, together we write,
Of boundless journeys beneath starlit night.

Mariner's Quill: Stories of the Shore

Upon the shore where sea meets sand,
A mariner's quill writes tales so grand.
Waves whisper secrets, old and wise,
Beneath the vast and starlit skies.

Each story flows like currents deep,
In salty air, they wake from sleep.
Tales of ships and stormy nights,
Of sirens' calls and magical flights.

From craggy cliffs, to coral bright,
The quill dances in the moon's soft light.
It captures dreams of those long gone,
In ink of twilight, tales are drawn.

The ocean hums its ancient song,
In rhythms where the brave belong.
With every stroke, the past unfolds,
In mariner's lore, adventure holds.

So gather 'round, both young and old,
For stories of the sea retold.
With every wave, new myths shall rise,
Through mariner's quill, the heart complies.

Fluid Tales in Saline Script

In liquid ink, the tales enscribe,
Of ocean's depths and tides that vibe.
The sea's embrace, a soft caress,
Each whispered wave, a gentle press.

Fluid tales in saline script,
By moonlit dreams, the words are gripped.
A sailor's heart, both fierce and warm,
Survives the storms, embraces charm.

Beneath the waves, in shadows cast,
Where secrets dance and sails are vast.
With every ebb and every flow,
New stories rise, like currents grow.

The shorelines blend with starry night,
As ink and water weave their light.
In every droplet, echoes ring,
Of mermaids' laughter, fish that sing.

So let the ocean's tales unfold,
In fluid ink, bright and bold.
For in each wave, a story lies,
Of life's great tides, where mystery flies.

The Enchanted Pen Beneath the Waves

Deep in the sea, where wonders dwell,
An enchanted pen casts its spell.
With strokes of magic on the scroll,
It weaves the tales of creatures' soul.

Ink from the depths, both bright and rare,
Scribes journeys taken, beyond compare.
Legends of tides and currents fierce,
Of hidden realms, the heart does pierce.

The pen glides through the watery realm,
Guided by dreams, it finds its helm.
From shipwrecked dreams to coral's glow,
Every word, like sea foam, flows.

Below the surface, stories blend,
Of ancient mariners, time does lend.
Each tale unfolds, like shells embraced,
In ocean's cradle, gently placed.

So close your eyes and drift away,
To where the pen and ocean play.
For in its ink, the world we seek,
Is found beneath the waves we speak.

Stories Told by the Moonlit Sea

In moonlit glow, the sea does weave,
A tapestry of tales we cleave.
With every wave, a story spun,
Of battles lost and victories won.

The salty breeze carries the sound,
Of laughter mixed with waves profound.
On sandy shores, under starlit sky,
The whispered tales of days gone by.

From fishermen's nets to pirate's treasure,
The tales unfold beyond all measure.
Secrets carried by the tides anew,
In every corner, a world of blue.

The moon, a witness to every plight,
Guides the hearts through the dark of night.
As ships sail forth with stories bold,
The sea gives voice to dreams retold.

So listen close, as waves do sigh,
The stories told shall never die.
In moonlit glow, where legends be,
The heart finds peace in the moonlit sea.

Ink-Soaked Secrets of the Sea

In shadows deep, where secrets lie,
The ocean whispers, soft and sly.
With ink-stained tales, the waves will weave,
A world of magic, hard to believe.

Beneath the swell, old stories breathe,
Of lost tomes and the dreams they bequeath.
The tides record each sigh and scream,
A salty parchment, a sailor's dream.

From sunken ships, their voices rise,
As whispers curl 'neath starlit skies.
Each drop a story, each wave a song,
In these blue depths, we all belong.

In coral caves where shadows dance,
The ink flows freely, a mystic trance.
Fairy tales drift on the current's hand,
Written in water, forever unplanned.

Dive into realms where legends fade,
Embrace the magic the ocean made.
The ink-soaked secrets, a treasure trove,
In every ripple, the stories rove.

The Depths of Ink and Dreams

In brackish waters, dreams take flight,
With ink-stained fingers, we pen the night.
Fantasies swirl in the ebb and flow,
Beneath the surface, where visions glow.

A sailor's heart, inked in despair,
Crafts words of longing, cast on the air.
His tales of love, of loss and fate,
Float on the currents, forever wait.

With every pulse of the restless sea,
The ink reveals what's meant to be.
Waves turn pages of yearning hearts,
In the depths, where sorrow departs.

The moonlight bathes the water bright,
Scripts of hope upon endless night.
Ink and dreams in a dance divine,
Together they weave the grand design.

Explore the dark where wonders gleam,
In the depths of ink, we dare to dream.
Lost in the vastness, yet never alone,
We find our stories, the sea our home.

Poetry Preserved in Brine

In jars of brine, the verses sleep,
Cradled by waves, their secrets keep.
With salty whispers, they call to me,
Eldritch rhymes of the deep blue sea.

Wrapped in kelp, where history lies,
Beneath the tides, forgotten sighs.
Every line, a tempest's grace,
Preserved in salt, time won't erase.

When storms arise, the words set free,
To dance upon the stormy spree.
Each drop a phrase, each wave a rhyme,
In the ocean's heart, they bide their time.

From ancient ships to mermaids' song,
The brine holds poems, forgotten long.
Echoes drift on a midnight breeze,
Whispering tales of the deep blue seas.

Unraveling secrets with every tide,
In poetry's embrace, the years abide.
With ink and brine, the verses shine,
In every creature, a tale divine.

Sirens' Verses Beneath the Surface

In twilight depths, the sirens sing,
Their melodies, a haunting fling.
In watery realms, they weave their spells,
Where every note its enchantment tells.

Echoes lost in a tranquil hush,
Where dreams are born in the ocean's rush.
With every word, a heart ensnares,
As tangled locks catch the salty airs.

Beneath the shimmer, secrets glint,
Each verse a promise, a lover's hint.
The surf's embrace, a tender hold,
In whispered verses, stories unfold.

Their lullabies drift on the night,
Guiding sailors with their light.
Yet beneath the song, danger lies,
As shadows play with the starry skies.

With every tide, their stories call,
In the depths of the sea, we lose it all.
Sirens' verses, both sweet and dire,
Ignite the heart with a burning fire.

Chasing Currents

In shadowed depths, we chase the light,
Where currents dance and dreams take flight.
Each ripple calls, a siren's song,
In whispered winds, we glide along.

The ocean's breath, a rhythmic beat,
Guides us through both calm and heat.
With every wave, a story flows,
Of tangled tides and hidden woes.

Beneath the surface, secrets hide,
In gales of fortune, we confide.
We ride the crests, defy the test,
In chasing currents, we find our rest.

Catching Words

Like fishing lines cast far and wide,
We anchor thoughts where dreams abide.
With nets of hope, we gather grace,
And weave our tales in time and space.

Each whispered word, a shimmering thread,
In tapestry where hearts are fed.
We gather verses, soft and clear,
As echoes linger, drawing near.

In every letter, magic grows,
A potion brewed from tales we chose.
With quills and ink, our spirits soar,
In catching words, we seek for more.

A Palette of Waves and Ink

With strokes of blue and hints of gold,
We paint the tales yet to be told.
Each wave a brush, the sea our muse,
In colors bright, the heart can't lose.

Beneath the foam, ideas bloom,
As artistry dispels the gloom.
Canvas of sand, and ocean's sigh,
Create a world where dreams can fly.

With every tide, the palette shifts,
In watercolor, our spirit lifts.
Through azure depths, our visions link,
A palette formed of waves and ink.

Poems that Swim in Briny Waters

In salty seas, our verses breathe,
Where whispers dwell and shadows weave.
Each poem swims through briny tides,
Upon the waves, our fate abides.

With every surge, a tale unfurls,
In depths unknown, a treasure swirls.
The ocean's heart, an endless book,
Where we explore with every look.

As currents pull, we glide and sway,
In briny waters, we find our way.
From starlit skies to moonlit seas,
Poems swim forth, a gentle breeze.

Liquid Ink from the Ocean's Heart

From depths of blue, the ink does flow,
A liquid tale of ebb and glow.
With every drop, a story spins,
Of ancient dreams and where we've been.

The ocean's heart, a fountain rare,
Where every wave holds whispered care.
We dip our pens in tides of lore,
In liquid ink, forevermore.

And as we write, the waters dance,
A shimmering realm where words enhance.
From salty breeze to tranquil part,
We draw our strength from ocean's heart.

Beneath the Surface: Tales Untold

In shadows deep where secrets lie,
Whispers float and dreams do sigh.
The ocean's heart, a treasure trove,
Holds stories deep as tales unfold.

With every wave, a secret song,
A voyage bound, where souls belong.
Beneath the churn of frothy crest,
The echoes dance, and hearts find rest.

The moonlit tide draws curious eyes,
Reflecting glimmers, stars in disguise.
Here legends swim in currents swift,
Beneath the waves, the tales will drift.

In kelp and coral, time stands still,
While dreams emerge on watery chill.
Through briny mists, the past intrigues,
As echoes whisper on the leagues.

So sail with me on this azure quest,
To chase the dreams that never rest.
For in each swell, a story waits,
Beneath the surface, beyond the gates.

A Dance of Ink and Driftwood

Upon a shore where sea meets sand,
The dance unfolds, as dreams are planned.
With ink of night on parchment white,
The waves compose a tale of light.

Driftwood treasures washed ashore,
Each fragment bears the tales of yore.
A cormorant dives, the sunbeams filter,
With every splash, the heart grows fonder.

The quill, it beckons with salty grace,
Where ink and ocean find their place.
Whirls of laughter rise and fall,
As stories weave a siren's call.

Across the pages, whispers twine,
In sandy verses, stars align.
The ink flows free like the rolling tide,
In driftwood tales, forever reside.

So let us dance on this timeless shore,
Where ink and driftwood dream of more.
A tapestry of ocean breath,
As waves and words weave life and death.

The Nautical Script of Sirens

On cliffs where echoes sing their strain,
The sirens weave their luring chain.
With voices sweet as summer's breeze,
They beckon forth the hearts that seize.

A script of salt and longing wait,
With every note, the tides sedate.
Beneath the stars, their lullabies,
A starlit path where mystery lies.

In shipwreck lore and phantom dreams,
Their call entangles, or so it seems.
With ink of twilight, the ocean writes,
A symphony of moonlit nights.

Through mist and foam, their secrets flow,
A sorcery that pulls us slow.
For sailors lost to heaven's beat,
In nautical scripts, our hearts repeat.

Approach the waves, let courage rise,
Where sirens sing beneath the skies.
In oceans deep, the stories find,
A script where love and fate entwined.

Deep-Sea Echoes in Liquid Letters

In depths where sunlight dares not dwell,
The echoing dreams begin to swell.
Letters dance in the water's hold,
Tales of yore and futures bold.

With each pulse, the currents weave,
A tapestry that hopes to cleave.
From shipwrecks lost in shadows cast,
The echoes call of seas long past.

Through barnacle blooms and coral light,
The whispers find their way to night.
In liquid letters laid with care,
The sea reveals its secrets rare.

With currents strong and tides that sway,
The ocean's heart beats night and day.
In echoes deep, the tales reside,
In liquid form, our hearts confide.

So dive with me into the blue,
Where echoes whisper what is true.
In depths unknown, we'll find our place,
In deep-sea echoes, we embrace.

Emerald Depths

In waters rich as emerald hues,
Where whispers dance and silence brews,
The secrets buried down below,
Invite the heart to gently row.

Beneath the waves, the shadows play,
In watery halls, they twist and sway,
A world where time begins to blend,
And each soft ripple seems to send.

The pearls of wisdom found in streams,
Are spun from every dreamer's dreams,
As currents sing a soothing song,
Entwined in magic, deep and strong.

Through kelp and coral, colors weave,
The ocean's heart, a warm reprieve,
Where every creature, great and small,
Carries whispers of a call.

In tranquil pools where moonlight glows,
The depth of nature's secrets shows,
An emerald world that breathes and sighs,
Each glance beneath its beauty lies.

Poetic Currents

When tides embrace the sandy shore,
And ink flows softly evermore,
The sea becomes a canvas wide,
Where ships of thought begin to glide.

Let waves of stories rise and swell,
Each crest a tale that waits to tell,
As water dances 'neath the sun,
Creating art where all are one.

The salty air, a muse unwound,
In every breath, new worlds are found,
With every surge, the heart expands,
And whispers flow like drifting sands.

A sonnet penned on ocean's page,
With every tide, the waves engage,
In rhythmic pulse, the verses swell,
A magic realm where all is well.

Let's ride the currents, feel the beat,
In harmony, we find our seat,
Together we will dream and soar,
As poets breathe the sea once more.

Ink Blots and Ocean Lotuses

In stillness blooms the ocean's heart,
With ink blots swirling, art's sweet start,
Lotuses rise with colors bright,
A canvas forged of purest light.

The quiet ebb recalls a tune,
Where dreams alight beneath the moon,
In every swirl, a story wakes,
A tapestry the sea remakes.

Brush strokes dance above the foam,
Creating bridges, finding home,
With every wave that breaks the shore,
The inked designs will ever soar.

As splashes form a written tale,
And bodies sway with each soft gale,
The lotuses in bloom will show,
What hidden wonders lie below.

With ocean's whispers, let us dream,
In vibrant hues, our spirits beam,
Where ink and blossom intertwine,
A world that waits, a chance divine.

Siren's Scribbles from the Water's Edge

Upon the rocks where sea foam plays,
The siren sings her haunting lays,
With ink and salt upon the page,
She writes of love, of loss, of rage.

Her verses flow like gentle tides,
In whispers soft, where magic hides,
Each scribble curls 'neath azure skies,
A glimpse of truth beyond the lies.

The ocean swells with every line,
While secrets weave through sea and brine,
In every note, a tale retold,
Of ancient treasures, brave and bold.

As twilight falls and stars embrace,
The waters shimmer, time and space,
Where sirens pen their songs in waves,
In depths of lore, the heart still craves.

So linger not, but dive right in,
Let rhythms pulse, let life begin,
For in the tales from water's edge,
The siren's voice forms a lovely pledge.

Beneath Echoing Waves: The Written Word

Beneath the waves, where silence sings,
Words drift like ships on gentle springs.
Stories swirl in the ocean's heart,
Crafted by souls, a world apart.

The pages turn in the watery light,
Each tale whispers, of day and night.
Dreams escape from ink and pen,
Beneath the waves, they dwell again.

In currents strong, the echoes rise,
Echoes of laughter, whispers, and sighs.
A tapestry woven through liquid thought,
In depths concealed, the wisdom sought.

With every wave, new tales unfold,
Of heroes brave and treasures old.
They flutter by like fish in the sea,
Beneath the waves, they call to me.

Currents of Imagination and Untold Stories

In currents swift, ideas flow,
Like tides that push and pull to grow.
Untold stories beneath the swell,
Whispers of magic in each shell.

Currents carry the dreams we weave,
In the ocean's depth, we dare believe.
Imagination soars, the heart takes flight,
As sunlight dances on waves of white.

With each crest, new visions spark,
Bright lanterns glowing in the dark.
Stories meander, twist and twine,
Emerging like pearls from the ocean's line.

The sea writes tales on a sandy shore,
Of ships that sailed and longed for more.
Every ripple, a promise, a guide,
In its embrace, we dream, collide.

The Deep Sea Poem: A Mermaid's Tale

In the deep blue, where shadows roam,
Lies a mermaid's heart, her secret home.
With silver scales that shimmer bright,
She sings to the stars, beneath the night.

Through coral reefs, her laughter rings,
Magic flows from the song she brings.
Each note a wish, each line a dream,
Carried away on the ocean's gleam.

She pens her tale on a seaweed scroll,
Of distant lands and the stories they hold.
In hidden caves, her whispers swell,
A deep sea poem, her soul to tell.

In moonlit waters, her heart takes flight,
Dancing with waves, a spirit of light.
Her melody echoes, both wild and free,
A mermaid's tale, a symphony of the sea.

Seafloor Scribbles: Tales of the Tides

In scribbles found on the seafloor's bed,
Tales of the tides, where the past is wed.
Shells collect memories, lost and found,
Their stories etched in the ocean's sound.

A starfish winks with a knowing smile,
Each brush of sand, a journey worthwhile.
Bubbles rise with laughter and lore,
Of sailors brave who walked the shore.

In swirling currents, secrets entangle,
Mysteries stir as the sea tides wrangle.
Who wrote the tales that the dolphins know?
Seafloor scribbles in a watery flow.

Brilliant hues of coral ignite,
A canvas alive with color and light.
The ocean's voice, soft yet grand,
Scribbles of wonder across the sand.

Echoes of the Deep: Verses from the Abyss

In shadows deep, where whispers dwell,
The ancient songs of water swell.
Creatures glide with silent grace,
In the vast and hidden place.

Beneath the veil of glimmering light,
Dreams of mariners take their flight.
Each ripple speaks of tales untold,
Of tempests fierce and treasures bold.

Voices call from deep below,
Where time and memory ebb and flow.
The currents twist with secrets kept,
In depths where sunlight rarely crept.

A journey through the azure sea,
To find what used to be so free.
The shadows play like fleeting sprite,
In the whispers of the night.

With every breath the ocean sighs,
Revealing truths beneath the skies.
In echoes of the deep abyss,
A world of wonder, lost in bliss.

A Poetry of Waves and Unwritten Secrets

The waves compose a symphony,
An orchestra of mystery.
Each crest, a word, each trough, a pause,
In nature's book, without a cause.

Shimmering sands caress the shore,
In rhythms that forever soar.
The tides hold secrets, old and wise,
Beneath the gaze of watchful skies.

With every swell, a story spins,
Of quiet depths where silence wins.
Ocean's heart beats strong and true,
A canvas vast and painted blue.

Each bubble bursts, a thought released,
In echoes soft, the mind finds peace.
The poetry of waves unfolds,
A tale of life the sea beholds.

In whispers sweet, the ocean speaks,
Of hopes and dreams, of hearts that seek.
In every wave, a future gleams,
A world alive with endless dreams.

Ink Dance Among the Coral Reef

Coral gardens bloom and sway,
In vibrant hues, where colors play.
Ink drops spill from artist's hand,
A dance of life on aquamarine land.

Fins flicker like a brush in flight,
Each movement caught in morning light.
Amidst the coral, stories rise,
A vivid tale beneath the skies.

Creatures dart in spirals tight,
A ballet beneath the moonlight.
Each swirl and twirl, a lively beat,
Where ocean whispers softly meet.

The current flows with artistry,
In depths where wonder roams so free.
An ink dance of the reef unfolds,
With cherished secrets to be told.

Among the corals, magic thrives,
In this world where beauty dives.
A symphony of life and hue,
An echo back to me and you.

Notes from the Ocean's Hidden Depths

Notes of the deep, a lullaby,
Sung by the waves that kiss the sky.
Voices drift on currents free,
Whispering tales of mystery.

In shadows cast by ancient tides,
Where sunlight fades and silence hides.
The ocean pens its secret scrolls,
In ink of brine, a story rolls.

Each note a treasure, softly placed,
In deepest dark, where dreams are chased.
The song of depths, a siren's call,
A promise written for us all.

With every ebb, a truth is shared,
In hidden depths, we find our dared.
Notes from the ocean's heart resound,
In each drop, a world profound.

The tides will turn, the stories wave,
In the ocean's arms, we find the brave.
From depths concealed, the notes arise,
A symphony beneath the skies.

Whispers of Ink Beneath the Sea

Beneath the waves, where shadows dwell,
Whispers of ink begin to swell.
Tales of mermaids, lost and free,
Caught in the currents, a mystery.

In the dark depths, secrets hide,
Inky trails where dreams collide.
A quill made from a sailor's bone,
Scribes the stories, all alone.

Shells like pages, soft and bright,
Glistening softly in silver light.
Echoes linger, soft and low,
In the tides that ebb and flow.

From shipwrecks old, the ink flows deep,
Carving legends where shadows creep.
Each bubble carries a whispered tale,
Of storms endured and hearts that sail.

With every stroke, the ocean sighs,
Filling the world with lullabies.
The ink beneath the sea will gleam,
As water weaves its timeless dream.

Secrets of a Submerged Pen

In crevices where silence breathes,
Lies a pen that wove the seas.
Its ink, a potion of dreams untold,
Whispers of magic in hues of gold.

Beneath the surface, twilight glows,
The pen scribing love no one knows.
As tides spin tales of distant years,
Each stroke unveils forgotten fears.

Echoes of sailors sing a tune,
To the rhythm of the silver moon.
Secrets flutter like a storm,
In the heart of waves, a mystic swarm.

Shells gather lines like pearls of lore,
Crafting letters from ancient shore.
The submerged pen, a keeper's hand,
Animating whispers of the land.

As ocean dances, the pen is still,
Yet its stories push the waves at will.
With every drop of liquid light,
The secrets of night begin their flight.

The Calligraphy of Tidal Dreams

In the twist of tides, the dreams cascade,
Calligraphy written, never to fade.
With waves as parchment, and foam as ink,
The ocean sings, urging hearts to think.

Swirling currents dance and swirl,
Tidal patterns begin to unfurl.
Every ripple a letter, every splash a word,
In the language of water, silently heard.

Beneath the surface, wonders bloom,
Where gels and shadows weave through gloom.
Scripted in bubbles, the stories rise,
Of sunlit seas and starry skies.

As the tides breathe, the world takes flight,
Under the glow of soft moonlight.
Waves roll in with a gentle sway,
Scribing dreams that drift away.

A sailor's heart listens close,
To whispers that the ocean chose.
In every swell, a journey gleams,
Through calligraphy of tidal dreams.

Scribing Stardust on Ocean Waves

On the horizon where water meets sky,
Stardust dances, sharp and spry.
Each wave a canvas, vast and clear,
Scribing stories for all to hear.

With every crest, a promise spun,
The ocean's spirit, a race begun.
Waves like brushstrokes, wild and free,
Painting the worlds we long to see.

Moonlight whispers, gentle and wise,
Glimmers of wonder where the twilight lies.
Ink of the cosmos spills and sings,
In the soft embrace of celestial wings.

A sailor writes with stars in hand,
Charting the shifts of a restless land.
The tide unfolds its hidden grace,
Scribing stardust's warm embrace.

In the salt-kissed air, dreams ignite,
Cast on the shores of endless night.
Through the waves' rhythmic, tender play,
We find our way, come what may.

Ink-Laden Tides

In shadows deep where secrets dwell,
The ink-laden tides weave a spell.
Whispers dance on the ocean breeze,
Carrying tales from the restless seas.

With every wave, a story born,
Of sailors lost and hearts that mourn.
Writings fade in the salty air,
Yet linger sweet in the salty fare.

A mermaid's song, a siren's call,
In fathoms deep where echoes fall.
The ink reveals what's left unsaid,
In currents where the brave dare tread.

Ink-laden tides with rhythm flow,
Telling of treasures carved below.
Each splash a line in an ancient tome,
Leading lost souls to their ocean home.

In silence woven, tales unfold,
Of mystic realms and glories told.
The tides still dance, they ebb, they flow,
In endless waltz with twilight glow.

Whispers from the Deep Sea Scrolls

Beneath the waves where shadows creep,
Lie scrolls forgotten, their stories deep.
The ocean hums a melodic tune,
A lullaby beneath the moon.

In currents swift, the whispers glide,
Of ancient lore where secrets bide.
The sea holds words in a tight embrace,
Capturing moments time can't erase.

With each wave's crest, a tale appears,
Of laughter lost and silent tears.
The deep sea scrolls begin to sing,
Of all the wonders oceans bring.

Forgotten dreams on currents drift,
In salty ink, they gently shift.
The whispers weave like seaweed spun,
In dances bright 'neath setting sun.

Oh, listen close, and you may find,
The stories left by humankind.
A tapestry of life awakes,
In whispers soft, the ocean breaks.

Secrets of the Ocean's Ink

In depths where shadows weave and twist,
Lie secrets penned in ocean mist.
The ink of waves on parchment flow,
With mysteries only deep can know.

Each drop a mark of legends past,
Of ships that sailed, memories cast.
The sea's great heart, a hidden tome,
With whispers soft, it calls us home.

In shimmering light, the stories leapt,
Of forgotten dreams the deep has kept.
Among the shells and coral bright,
The tales await in the fading light.

Oft in the night, you'll hear their plea,
Echoes of lives that longed to be free.
The ocean writes with salty grace,
In every wave's embrace, a trace.

So dive within, and you shall see,
The secrets wrapped in mystery.
For in the ink of oceans vast,
Lie echoes of stories unsurpassed.

Ephemeral Waves of Thought

Like whispers soft, the waves will rise,
Ephemeral thoughts beneath the skies.
They dance with grace upon the shore,
Leaving footprints that are no more.

With each crest breaking, tales take flight,
In fleeting moments, both day and night.
The sea is full of wisps and dreams,
In every splash, imagination gleams.

What once was clear, now dims away,
As thoughts dissolve at the end of day.
Yet in their ebb, they softly speak,
Of silent hopes, the heart's mystique.

The tide retreats but leaves a hint,
Of everything we fear and stint.
Ephemeral waves of thought cascade,
In every ripple, a memory made.

So let the ocean guide your mind,
Through waves of grace, be unconfined.
For in each surge, a truth appears,
Unwritten lines, released from fears.

Echoes of the Maritime Muse

In twilight whispers, the sea does sigh,
A melody woven, 'neath the vast sky.
Each wave a story, soft and untold,
Where secrets linger, both timid and bold.

A sailor's lament, a breeze through the trees,
The echoing chorus of salt on the breeze.
Crimson horizons, where day meets the night,
The muse of the ocean ignites the light.

With shells as our canvas, we craft the refrain,
In tides and in moonlight, joy mingles with pain.
The song of the deep, both haunting and free,
A timeless connection, the heart of the sea.

As stars spin their tales in the midnight expanse,
The waves dance in rhythm, in an eternal trance.
From shipwrecks of yore to the dreams yet to sail,
We find in the depths, our stories unveil.

Ocean's Heart Penning Poetry

Ink from the waters, the ocean does spill,
Crafting its lore with an indomitable will.
Upon parchment of waves, each ripple inscribed,
A ballad of mermaids, of longing, described.

Beneath the azure, where shadows entwine,
A symphony hums, in a rhythm divine.
The tides weave their verses, both fierce and serene,
In currents of dreams, where the heart lies between.

With starlit reflections, the sonnets ascend,
The ocean, a poet, its secrets extend.
From seagull's soft cry to the thunderous roar,
Each sound an enigma, forever to explore.

Whispers of sailors who lost their brave quest,
In depths of despair, the sea held them best.
For in every heartbeat, the waters compose,
A narrative timeless, where wonder still grows.

Scribbles from Tide's Embrace

The canvas of sand, with tide's fleeting kiss,
Bears secrets and sketches, a moment of bliss.
With laughter and whispers, the shore comes alive,
As children of ocean, in harmony thrive.

Each grain is a memory, small yet profound,
A footprint, a treasure, among the surround.
Tide pools hold poems of life and decay,
Where silence holds stories of night and of day.

Amidst the driftwood, the tales intertwine,
Of storms that have passed, in the sun's gentle shine.
With every new wave that erases our trails,
The sea writes our journey, where laughter prevails.

And echoes of wishes float far on the breeze,
While hearts beat in time with the rhythmic seas.
In nature's embrace, with spirit and grace,
We scribble our lives in the ocean's soft trace.

The Language of Shell and Ink

In whispers of shells, the ocean's heart glows,
A language of beauty, in each ebb and flow.
With whispers of foam, and secrets of sand,
The heart speaks in colors, both gentle and grand.

With ink made of brine, and quill from the shore,
We capture the magic, the legends of yore.
As waves throw their laughter, in rhythm they sing,
The tales of the sea, in their salt-soaked wing.

Midnight blue currents, where shadows take flight,
A dance of the daring, beneath pale moonlight.
In every soft crash, a story takes form,
Of adventures and dreams, within nature's warm.

The journey continues, on this boundless page,
With every new wave, we release, we engage.
The heart of the ocean, our ink and our dream,
In shells, in the whispers, we find our theme.

Tales of the Abyss: Written in Water

In depths below where shadows swirl,
The secrets dance in ocean's whirl.
Each drop a story, faintly told,
Of ancient wonders and dreams of gold.

The siren's song calls with a sigh,
To wanderers lost, who dare to try.
In currents strong, fate weaves its thread,
Through tangled kelp where light has fled.

With every wave, the past returns,
A flickering flame that never burns.
Below the tide, lost treasures gleam,
In murky depths, life flows like a dream.

The surface glimmers, calm and bright,
Yet underneath, the shadows byte.
Each ripple holds a whispered tale,
Of courage found, and hearts that sail.

So dive into the waters deep,
Where dreams and truths forever seep.
For in the abyss, all things are clear,
Magic and mystery, always near.

Ocean's Muse: The Scribe of the Sea

Upon the shore, where waves embrace,
The ocean's muse finds her place.
With quill in hand, she starts to write,
Of moonlit nights and starry sights.

Her ink is drawn from depths unknown,
Reflecting hearts that've ever grown.
She pens the tales of sailors bold,
Of storms that rage and legends old.

Each line a whisper, soft as spray,
Of mermaids' songs that fade away.
Her parchment woven from the tide,
A masterpiece where fancies glide.

She writes of love that would not yield,
Of adventurers in battles healed.
In every word, a heartbeat sings,
A symphony of ocean kings.

So read the waves and hear their call,
For every moment holds it all.
In ocean's depths, the stories swell,
Of life, of magic, woven well.

Letters from the Coral Kingdom

In vibrant hues, the corals glow,
As gentle currents ebb and flow.
From hidden thrones where silence reigns,
The ocean shares its rich refrains.

With every stroke of sea-folk's brush,
Beneath the waves, there's always hush.
They pen their letters, soft and slow,
To distant lands, where dreamers go.

"Dear friend," they write, "the tides are kind,
With treasures vast, our hearts entwined.
The dolphins dance, the seagrass sways,
In sunlight's glow, we spend our days."

Each script a tale of joy and plight,
Of shadows cast in fleeting light.
A world alive beneath the foam,
In every stroke, a glimpse of home.

So hear the whispers from below,
As waves and tides together flow.
For in their letters, truth is spun,
A love letter to everyone.

Seashells Whispers: A Poetic Voyage

Upon the shore, the seashells lay,
Emblems of journeys, lost in spray.
Each whisper tells of lands afar,
Where tides and dreams both rise and spar.

A conch may speak of storms once brewed,
Of tempest wild, and fortunes skewed.
While delicate sand dollars gleam,
Echoes of laughter spark a dream.

In every shell, a secret stays,
Hushed by the ocean's murmured ways.
The grains of sand, like time, slip past,
Memories held, forever cast.

So wander where the tide has kissed,
Each shell a fragment of the mist.
A narrative of waves set free,
A poetic voyage, just for thee.

Collect these whispers, treasures dear,
For in their songs, the world is clear.
Embrace the voyage, ride the swell,
In nature's art, hear every shell.

Reflections in the Tidal Pool

In the quiet gloom of the tide,
Little creatures hidden inside,
Mirrors dance in the water's embrace,
Each ripple tells tales of the place.

Seaweed whispers secrets of old,
Touched by sunlight, gleaming like gold,
Waves hum soft songs of the deep,
Guarding the dreams that the ocean keeps.

Shells hold echoes of storms long past,
Stories of sailors, their shadows cast,
With every glance, a memory flows,
In the tidal pool, life gently grows.

Bubbles rise, like thoughts in the air,
Moments caught in the watery stare,
Reflections weave through salt and foam,
Each glance shared, a journey home.

As twilight cloaks the world in grey,
The tidal pool holds night at bay,
With moonlight painting a silver sheet,
Nature's magic, a wondrous feat.

Ocean's Paper: A Canvas of Waves

The ocean sprawls like an open book,
Its pages churn with every nook,
Waves scribble tales on the sandy shore,
A dance of stories, forevermore.

Seagulls sketch arcs in clear blue skies,
In the margins, laughter and sighs,
Each crest and fall, a line unfurled,
Tales of hidden treasures, a world.

Salt and spray paint the sea's great prose,
Ink from the depths where currents pose,
Words crafted by the whispering tide,
Ebullient melodies flow and glide.

Footprints mark where dreams have been,
Scribbled thoughts of what lies within,
With every ebb, new chapters bloom,
The narrative flows, a vibrant loom.

Paper of the ocean, vast and wide,
Crafted in colors, a wondrous tide,
Here among the waves, we find our way,
In the heart of the sea, we learn to play.

Serenade of the Seas: Ink and Imagination

In the heart of the ocean blue,
Where dreams sail freely with each view,
An ink-filled quill writes melodies,
Serenades whispered by the seas.

The waves beat softly a rhythmic tune,
Beneath the glow of the silver moon,
Each rise and fall, a note in the air,
Crafting symphonies without a care.

Clouds gather close, a canvas vast,
Imagination flows with currents fast,
Seashells gather stories, old yet bright,
In this grand concert of day and night.

Against the rocks, the dreams collide,
Ebbing and flowing, like fate's own guide,
With every splash, a whisper of lore,
Ink and imagination forever soar.

So listen closely, let the waves sing,
In every crash, hear the joy they bring,
A serenade to the hearts that roam,
In the ocean's embrace, we find our home.

Riptides of Reflection and Rhyme

In riptides where the shadows play,
Thoughts are tossed like leaves in May,
With every swirl, a story spins,
Echoes of laughter, where it begins.

The sea reflects the sky's delight,
Mirroring stars on a canvas night,
In the depths, our secrets are bound,
Tidal currents, where dreams are found.

Waves whisper softly, a rhythmic thrill,
With every crash, time stands still,
Riptides pulling the heart so near,
Luring us close with nothing to fear.

As moonlight dances on liquid glass,
Each moment captured, we let it pass,
Reflections ripple in melodic rhyme,
Riding the riptides, transcending time.

So let the ocean cradle your soul,
In waves of reflection, we become whole,
For in every swell, life's wonders chime,
Riptides of wisdom in rhythm and rhyme.

Beneath the Waves

In depths where dreams and shadows play,
The whispers of the sea drift away.
Mysteries swirl in a cerulean embrace,
Guardians of secrets, in silence, they trace.

Moonlight kisses the water's face,
Echoes of wonders in an endless space.
Fish dart like thoughts in the vibrant blue,
Beneath the surface, all feels anew.

Stories Arise

From depths of the ocean, tales begin,
Of sailors lost and the laughter akin.
Each wave, a page in the book of the sea,
Spinning stories of what used to be.

With every swell, memories bloom,
Selkies and mermaids dance in the gloom.
The tide carries whispers to distant shores,
Leaving echoes of legends that time restores.

Letters from the Trench of Time

In silent chambers where past meets present,
Letters unfurl with a wisdom effervescent.
Ink drips like raindrops on ancient sand,
Each word a treasure from a faraway land.

Echoes resonate in the still of the night,
Fingers trace paths of memories in flight.
History whispers in the hush of the breeze,
Binding the ages with delicate ease.

Waves Whispering the Written Word

The ocean's breath carries tales that endure,
Each ripple, a message, both gentle and pure.
Seashells hold secrets of love and of war,
Waves whisper softly, inviting us more.

In frothy embraces, they weave and they sway,
Drawing us closer, no words can convey.
Their language, a ballet of rhythm and rhyme,
Telling us stories that transcend time.

Shoreline Scribbles and Maritime Dreams

On sandy pages where footprints remain,
Dreams are inscribed in the sun and the rain.
With seashells for pens, tales weave through the day,
Creating a world that will never decay.

The horizon beckons with colors so bright,
As day fades to dusk, giving way to night.
Stars like scribbles scatter across the dome,
Guiding the sailor, leading him home.

Maritime Dreams

In the heart of the sea, dreams drift and sail,
Carried by currents, they whisper a tale.
Together with starlight, they dance on the wave,
Inviting the brave and the lost to be saved.

With each gentle swell, hopes rise and then fall,
The rhythm of life, a magical call.
Beneath moonlit skies, where the wild waters gleam,
The ocean cradles all within its dream.

Tidal Tales of a Forgotten Realm

On shores where whispers ride the breeze,
Old stories dwell beneath the seas.
With shells that sing of ages past,
And tides that tell of sailors cast.

Beneath the waves, a kingdom sleeps,
Where time is lost and silence weeps.
In currents deep, the secrets curl,
Of heartaches spun in a watery whirl.

The coral forests softly sway,
In hues of dreams that drift away.
As echoes call from depths unknown,
Longing for the hearts they've shown.

In every crest, a tale unfolds,
Of daring deeds and treasures bold.
Yet shadows loom, both fierce and bright,
Within the depths of day and night.

The tides may turn, the storms may roar,
But still the tales are told on shore.
Where dust meets sand and time stands still,
The ocean's heart beats strong and will.

Inked Waves Cradle Secrets

With quills dipped deep in ocean's hue,
We write the tales that drift and brew.
Each wave a line, each storm a plot,
Inked with the dreams that time forgot.

The parchment glistens, rich and old,
As salty winds breathe stories bold.
A whisper here, a shanty there,
In every mark, a soul laid bare.

Beneath the moon, the shadows dance,
As inked waves weave their timeless romance.
With every stroke, a life reclaims,
The mysteries tied to ancient names.

Around the shores where legends creep,
In quiet hours, the secrets sleep.
Yet inked in dreams, they rise anew,
A story told, forever true.

With every tide, a twist and turn,
To ink the waves, for hearts that yearn.
In every drop, in every trace,
A glimpse of love, an endless chase.

Mermaid's Essence in Every Stroke

In whispers where the seaweed sways,
A mermaid laughs in ocean's plays.
Her essence glows in colors bright,
As stars ignite the canvas night.

With every brush, a tale she'll spin,
Of hidden depths and worlds within.
Her laughter ripples, echoing clear,
As art becomes the song we hear.

Each stroke a wave, each splash a sigh,
As time flows on, like sunlight's cry.
In watery depths, her heart will bloom,
Casting light away from gloom.

The canvas knows her ancient lore,
Of kingdoms lost and myths of yore.
With swirling hues, she paints the soul,
A depth of dreams to make us whole.

For every wave that joins the shore,
A mermaid's song forevermore.
The essence of her spirit thrives,
In every brush, the ocean strives.

The Depths of Written Mystique

In twilight realms where shadows blend,
The depths of stories never end.
With inked emotions, deep and vast,
Descend with me to echoes cast.

Each page a wave, a pull, a tide,
As secrets deep within abide.
Whispers linger, tales retrace,
The dance of time, a sweet embrace.

The lantern's glow on parchment spills,
Awakening the haunting thrills.
With each new word, a life shall rise,
From depths unknown, 'neath starry skies.

In currents dark, the truth reveals,
The weight of words, the heart that feels.
For stories breathe and drift away,
Yet linger close, in dreams they stay.

The written mystique, a lullaby,
Carried forth by the evening sigh.
So let us tread where few have gone,
In depths of prose, we'll find our dawn.

Dreamcatcher of the Deep

In the hush of twilight's breath,
Where shadows dance with dreams of death,
The ocean's whispers softly creep,
To weave a catch of night's deep sleep.

Stars above like fireflies gleam,
Their light reflects a silken dream,
While ocean depths hum tales untold,
In currents warm and waters cold.

Ghostly ships in moonlit sway,
On whispered tides, they drift away,
With nets of silver, catch the hue,
Of dreams that linger, pure and true.

Tales of love and loss do blend,
In every wave, a message send,
The heart's desires cast as bait,
A timeless search, a twist of fate.

So when the night begins to fall,
Listen close, let silence call,
For in the deep, dreams softly weave,
A tapestry of what we believe.

Tales in the Water's Embrace

Where ripples form a tapestry,
The water holds its mysteries,
With every wave and subtle flow,
A tale of old begins to grow.

The gentle breeze through weeping willows,
Whispers secrets in soft billows,
Songs of mermaids, lost in time,
Echo through the silent rhyme.

A twilight dance upon the lake,
In every splash, a chance to wake,
To stories of the brave and bold,
Of treasures found and legends told.

The moon reflects a silver dance,
Inviting all to take a chance,
To dive into the depths of night,
And seek the wonders out of sight.

In water's grasp, we find our peace,
Each glimpse a puzzle, a sweet release,
For every tide that comes to play,
Brings forth a tale to light our way.

Enchanted Waters of Expression

Beneath the surface, dreams once shy,
Awake in colors, bold and spry,
The water spills its stories bright,
In liquid realms of soft twilight.

With every drop, emotions flow,
In swirls of laughter, joy, and woe,
An artist's brush upon the stream,
Creating worlds where visions gleam.

The fish leap high, like words unspoken,
As melodies of silence broken,
In gurgling laughter, echoes swell,
Each splash a verse, each ripple, a spell.

The sun dips low, a golden hue,
Capturing whispers, fresh and new,
As twilight paints with brush of light,
The canvas of the coming night.

So dive within, let spirits rise,
Embrace the magic, reach for skies,
For in these waters, art unfolds,
Enchanting truths, forever holds.

Penning the Oceans' Reverie

With quill in hand, I sail the seas,
As oceans hum their melodies,
Each wave a line upon my page,
In liquid ink, I find my sage.

Winds of fortune guiding me,
Through tempests fierce, I roam so free,
In every storm, a story spins,
Each crest and trough, where life begins.

Shells and relics whisper past,
Echoes of moments, long since cast,
In every grain of sand I trace,
The tales of love, and loss, and grace.

This ocean vast, a heart laid bare,
A sanctuary, beyond compare,
For where the tide meets land's embrace,
I pen the dreams that time can't erase.

So let me drift on salty air,
And find the truths that linger there,
In every swell, a story untold,
In every breath, the sea, so bold.

The Siren's Scribe

In shadows deep where secrets dwell,
A scribe appears with tales to tell.
Her ink flows like the ocean's tide,
A voice of dreams that won't subside.

With every stroke a melody,
Of ships and hearts, of destiny.
The waves they beckon, softly call,
To men who dare to brave it all.

But beware the charm of her sweet song,
For paths entwined can lead to wrong.
In whispered tones she weaves her art,
Yet leaves a toll upon the heart.

A journal filled with hopes and fears,
Preserved in ink, not dried by tears.
For every tale a price must be,
The scribe will seek what sets you free.

So gather round, hold tales in thrall,
And listen close to fortune's call.
In moonlit nights beneath the skies,
Remember well the siren's lies.

Currents of Lost Lore

In twilight's grasp, the stories fade,
Of ancient times and the price they paid.
The river flows with whispers low,
Of currents deep where secrets grow.

Beneath the surface, shadows twine,
With echoes of a grand design.
The fish they leap with tales to share,
Of warriors bold and lovers rare.

Yet still the depths conceal the truth,
In currents swift, the lure of youth.
As flowers bloom on riverbanks,
Beware the flow, lest wisdom shrinks.

A tale untold, a fable lost,
In ripples soft, at what a cost.
The lore once bright now cloaked in shade,
In hidden waves, their meaning swayed.

So paddle forth and heed the stream,
For every dream is not what it seems.
Through trials faced, let spirits soar,
And find the truth in lore before.

Beneath the Moon's Liquid Gaze

Under moonlight's silvery glow,
The world transforms, a gentle show.
Ripples dance on waters pale,
As night unfurls her whispered tale.

The stars ignite, a celestial cheer,
Guiding hearts, drawing near.
With every flicker, dreams take flight,
In shadows wrapped, the thrill of night.

But hark, the wind carries a sigh,
Of wishes lost, as time slips by.
A tapestry of hopes and fears,
Woven soft with moonlit tears.

Beneath the gaze of night's embrace,
A fleeting chance, a moment's grace.
The waters shimmer, a silver stream,
Reflecting all our lost daydreams.

So linger here where silence waits,
In dreams unleashed, open the gates.
For under moon's soft, tender plea,
Life flows freely, oh, let it be.

Letters from the Abyss

In darkness deep, where shadows creep,
Lie letters laced with secrets steep.
From silent depths of ocean's heart,
A tale begins, a lover's part.

Each parchment worn, a relic lost,
Whispers of love, oh, what a cost.
With ink of night and paper thin,
These words of longing, where to begin?

Through storms and waves, they brave the night,
These letters drift from wrong to right.
For each embrace a sorrow born,
As tides of fate their spirits scorn.

Yet still they resonate in dreams,
In ocean's pulse, the heart redeems.
From sirens' call to sailor's woe,
Each letter sings of joy and sorrow.

So cast your thoughts where waters sigh,
And read the truth beneath the sky.
For in these letters, love persists,
A haunting echo, in the abyss.

Deep Waters

In shadows where the sirens sing,
The heart of ocean whispers low.
With every ripple, secrets cling,
In depths where only dreamers go.

Darkness folds the fading light,
A dance of creatures, soft and shy.
Beneath the waves, a world ignites,
Where time swims backward, time slips by.

The currents weave their timeless tales,
Of mariners lost and treasures found.
A soft lament in the wind prevails,
In silence deep, where dreams abound.

From coral palaces to caves untold,
A hush resides where echoes play.
In deep waters, stories unfold,
In shimmering hues of blue and gray.

Deeper Words

In the stillness of the night,
Where stars like jewels brightly gleam,
Words sink deeper, taking flight,
In whispers carried on a dream.

From depths of thought, profound and wide,
They swirl like tides beneath the mind.
In verses, truth and fears abide,
In ink, the soul's reflections find.

With every stroke, a journey starts,
Through caverns rich with hidden lore.
Each syllable, a work of art,
Emerging from the ocean's core.

They dance upon the paper's sheet,
A lantern glow in darkest seas.
In deeper words, our spirits meet,
A chorus sung by ocean breeze.

Ink Currents of the Marine Heart

In the gentle sway of waves,
The ink flows deep like ocean's breath.
From pens, the marine heart raves,
With stories spun from life and death.

Beneath the surface, tales will swell,
Of sailors brave and monsters grand.
The ink reflects a watery spell,
Of voyages across the land.

Drifting down where shadows play,
The words weave magic, bright and bold.
In tides of ink, they find their way,
To script the secrets of the old.

With every stroke, the oceans part,
A symphony of written dreams.
These ink currents, a marine heart,
Flow steadily through endless streams.

The Lurid Wave of Literary Tides

Beneath the moon's soft, silvery sigh,
Literature swells like ocean's might.
Waves of words both low and high,
Carry the mind on a thrilling flight.

Each tide unearths the tales once lost,
In swell and crash, concepts collide.
What thought begets, what dreams are tossed,
In the lurid wave, we shall confide.

Surging forth with tempests wild,
Through pages torn and eyes agleam.
Each passage penned, a playful child,
In stormy seas of thought's deep scheme.

The literary tides, both fierce and kind,
Bring forth the visions dimly seen.
With every surge, we seek to find,
The story woven in the sheen.

Songs of the Deep and Scales of Ink

In the ocean's depths, a melody calls,
Songs of the deep, where treasures lie.
Through vibrant hues, the silence falls,
Carrying whispers from a distant sky.

Each note cascades like rolling waves,
Scales of ink that shimmer bright.
With every breath, the ocean saves,
A harmony of dark and light.

The sirens sing of battles fought,
In ballads deep, where legends thrive.
Each lyric, like a net, is brought,
To capture hearts and keep them alive.

In swirls of azure, tales weaved tight,
The songs arise, a soothing balm.
Through depths unknown, they take their flight,
With scales of ink, a dreamlike calm.

Inked Dreams of Siren Songs

Beneath the sea, where shadows dwell,
Whispers of dreams begin to swell.
In ink and heartbeat, stories rise,
Siren songs weave through the skies.

With every splash, a tale unfolds,
Of ships and treasures, brave and bold.
A quill to trace the ocean's breath,
Each line a dance with life and death.

The horizon bends, as stars ignite,
Illuminating the darkest night.
In waters deep, secrets lie,
As echoes linger and softly sigh.

In dreams we sail on silver waves,
Finding the courage in hidden caves.
For every heart that dares to dive,
The ink of hope will still survive.

So let the tides of fate embark,
On paths where only dreamers spark.
With inked dreams and siren songs,
In the ocean's arms, the soul belongs.

The Ocean's Call: Writing with Waves

The ocean calls with a rhythmic sound,
A gentle roar, where thoughts unbound.
With each wave's crash upon the shore,
A world of wonder waits to explore.

Pen in hand, I chase the tide,
Where secrets and stories gently hide.
As foam and fervor meet the land,
Words swirl like shells in soft, warm sand.

Every ripple echoes, every sigh,
Breath of the sea in the moonlit sky.
I capture dreams on parchment bright,
Letting the waves guide my flight.

With salt-kissed air that speaks of grace,
I wander the shores of time and space.
Each stroke a memory, each line a prayer,
Written in whispers, carried with care.

Thus bound to the ocean's endless pull,
My heart finds rest, my spirit full.
In writing with waves, forever free,
I pen the tides that call to me.

Verses of the Blue: Scribing in Tides

In the cradle of blue, the verses dance,
Rippling the surface, a serendipitous chance.
With each gentle swell, a word takes flight,
Scribing the echoes of day and night.

The sun-kissed foam wears a crown of dreams,
As I gather the stories from murmuring streams.
With ink in hand, I trace the shore,
Crafting the tales of sea's eternal lore.

Here, whispers ripple in timeless flow,
Every tide tells what we need to know.
In the depths of blue, mysteries unfold,
A treasure of verses, worth more than gold.

Seashells hum of sailors' plight,
While the sky blushes with fading light.
With winds as guides, I sail my pen,
To capture the magic now and again.

Amongst the waves, my thoughts drift free,
Writing the tides, becoming the sea.
With every verse, a piece of my heart,
In the ocean's embrace, I find my art.

Nautical Quests and Poetic Finds

A sailor's quest upon the brine,
Where stars align and fates entwine.
With compass set, I dare to roam,
Each word a wave that pulls me home.

The hull creaks softly like a bard,
For every journey has its guard.
In open skies and salty air,
I pen my fears and joys laid bare.

From misty dawn to twilight's glow,
The ink flows freely, as feelings grow.
Each treasure found in depths unknown,
Leads to the heart, where dreams are sown.

With nautical maps and poetic signs,
I anchor my soul in tangled lines.
The sea whispers secrets, so profound,
In its melodic depths, I'm spellbound.

Exploring horizons both near and far,
The ocean's heart is my guiding star.
In nautical quests, my spirit sings,
For poetry lives where adventure brings.

The Inked Abyss

In shadows deep, where secrets dwell,
A tale is spun, a whispered spell.
The ink flows thick, the tide is high,
To mirror dreams that dance and fly.

With quills like stars, we write our fate,
A parchment boat awaits the date.
The abyss beckons, dark and vast,
Where echoes of the past are cast.

An ocean heart, forever bound,
In currents deep, our truths are found.
We carve our names on every wave,
A legacy, the brave shall save.

In depths where light begins to fade,
The ink of night, our hearts parade.
With every stroke, a story penned,
The abyss calls, our journeys blend.

So let us sail on paper seas,
With wild tales carried by the breeze.
In inked abyss, our fears arise,
But courage sparks beneath the skies.

Seafoam Words

Whispers float upon the tide,
As seafoam words in oceans glide.
They tell of storms, of peace, of strife,
Each salty wave, a tale of life.

With every crest, a secret shared,
The rhythm of the sea has dared.
To write in froth, in shimmering light,
Of dreams alive, of fancies bright.

A sailors ink, the ocean's pen,
Crafting stories time again.
From tangled shores where mermaids sing,
To fading dusk, when night takes wing.

Each tidal turn, a line refined,
In seafoam words, our souls entwined.
Together bound, through storm and sun,
With whispered tales, our hearts outrun.

So cast your nets in waters deep,
And gather words for dreams to keep.
In seafoam's grasp, both wild and free,
We find our voice, we claim the sea.

Tidal Tales: Stories of the Deep

From ocean depths, where shadows breathe,
The tidal tales, the hidden weaves.
With every wave, the stories swell,
In whispered currents, secrets dwell.

A treasure spark, a siren's cry,
On briny wind, our hopes will fly.
From kelp and shells, our myths are spun,
In ocean's heart, our journey's begun.

They speak of storms and hidden shores,
Of ancient ships and legends' roars.
Each gentle wave, a voice that calls,
In tidal tales, the memory falls.

Beneath the moon, the waters gleam,
Where dreams entwine in silver stream.
Through deep abyss and coral bright,
The stories whisper in the night.

So let us delve in seas unknown,
And in the depths, our spirits hone.
For in these tides, our fates will weave,
The stories sung, we won't believe.

The Scribe of Sea and Sand

Upon the shore, where waves embrace,
The scribe of sea and sand finds grace.
With every grain, a tale is told,
Of sailors fierce and treasures bold.

In twilight hues, the ink will flow,
As tides conspire, and breezes blow.
A parchment rolled, beneath the skies,
The stories hidden, the heart's replies.

With whispers soft, the sands recite,
Of fleeting dreams, of endless nights.
The crashing waves, a symphony,
As whispers float in harmony.

From pearls of wisdom washed ashore,
The scribe will weave forevermore.
With quill in hand, beneath the sun,
The songs of sea and sand are spun.

So wander close, where waters meet,
And in their depths, your heart will greet.
The scribe will tell, the ink will flow,
In sea and sand, our tales will grow.

Whalesong and Written Tides

In deep blue waters, echoes play,
A whalesong drifts, a sweet ballet.
With every note, a story flows,
Of ancient hearts, and love that grows.

The written tides, they turn and swirl,
With each soft wave, our dreams unfurl.
In rhythmic dance, we find our place,
In oceans wide, we leave our trace.

The deep calls forth, with voice so grand,
In whalesong's swell, we understand.
A melody in currents strong,
Where spirits soar, forever long.

In verses soft, the sea's embrace,
We write our tales in every space.
Through whispered tides and ocean's sigh,
Our hearts will soar, and never die.

So let us cast our nets and dream,
With whalesong sweet, in moonlit gleam.
In written tides, our stories sing,
In harmony, the waves take wing.

When Currents Carry Pen and Paper

In the hush of twilight's grace,
Waves dance lightly to a tune.
Whispers of forgotten tales,
Flow through shadows of the moon.

With every stroke, the ink takes flight,
Sketching dreams upon the tide.
Currents weave through realms unknown,
Where thoughts and fantasies abide.

Sails are set on paper seas,
Navigating through the night.
A compass made of word and breeze,
Guiding hearts towards the light.

Journey forth through mist and mist,
Chasing stars past silver gleam.
The world unfolds within this swirl,
Where every drop ignites a dream.

Let phantoms guide the wandering quill,
As tides turn with a gentle sigh.
In silence, ink begins to spill,
Painting visions in the sky.

Each page a glimpse of ocean's song,
Crafted by the currents' pull.
Forever will these stories throng,
Mirroring the heart's deep lull.

Inked Seashells and Writings of the Deep

Beneath the waves where secrets sleep,
Inked seashells cradle tales untold.
Their whispers rise with every sweep,
Of tides that shift and dreams unfold.

A treasure trove of stories new,
Each curl and twist a written sign.
In the depths, where spirits flew,
Writings linger, soft and fine.

From coral thrones to sunken ships,
Ghostly remnants of ancient lore.
Lurking depths where wonder slips,
Ink flows free on ocean's floor.

Every wave, a turn of phrase,
Every bubble tells a tale.
In friendly currents, dreams amaze,
As thought and water gently sail.

Let the legacies of the sea,
Echo through the ageless night.
Inked seashells sing of harmony,
As darkness mingles with the light.

Fathoms of Fantasy: Poems from Below

In fathoms deep where shadows dwell,
A world awakes in silent bloom.
Coral gardens weave their spell,
While echoes rise from ocean's womb.

From lantern fish to starlit skies,
Each creature paints a mystic view.
Beneath the surface, magic lies,
Awaiting hearts to pull it through.

Through kelp forests and tranquil bays,
Ink drips from the heart's own verse.
Tales of wonder greet the waves,
As dreams converge in ocean's purse.

Submerged realms of joy and pain,
Fantasies that shift and shape.
In the depths, a world unchained,
Invites the brave to boldly scrape.

Let every poet's heart now dive,
Where wonders wait in shy repose.
In fathoms deep, our dreams arrive,
And whisper what the ocean knows.

The Mermaid's Ink and Ocean's Verse

In moonlit waves, the mermaid sings,
Her voice a lure, her spirit bright.
With every note, enchantment clings,
To shores where dreams and shadows fight.

Her ink flows with the tides in time,
Caressing parchment, soft and old.
Verses dance in rhythm and rhyme,
As stories of the sea unfold.

The ocean's breath, a gentle muse,
Invites the heart to freely roam.
In her embrace, none can refuse,
The call to wander far from home.

Rippled dreams on water's page,
The mermaid's craft a rare delight.
Her tales awaken every age,
A beacon through the starry night.

So take the plunge, let ink take flight,
With each adventure, find your place.
In ocean's verse, the heart ignites,
Where every soul finds gentle grace.